길 위에서
On the Road

지성·감성의 메타언어
조선문학사시인선.937

길 위에서
On the Road

이원로 제 58 시집
The 58th Poetry Book of Lee Won-Ro

조선문학사

Contents 차례

Prologue 프롤로그
Beyond the Fence 울타리 밖 ·················· 10

Part I 제1부
Achievement 성취

Achievemen 성취 ···················· 14
Sensor 센서 ························ 16
Human and Beast 사람과 짐승 ·········· 18
Intuition 직감 ······················ 20
The Void 허공 ····················· 22
The Mysterious Forest 신비의 숲 ········· 24
Reaction 반응 ······················ 26
Transcendence 초월 ·················· 28
Small Joyst 작은 기쁨 ················ 30
Essential Desire 본질적 욕구 ············ 32
Bound and Entangled 묶임과 얽힘 ········ 34

Part II 제2부
Thaw 해동

Milestone 이정표 ·· 38
Passing Through the Tunnel 터널 통과 ·········· 40
Shadow 그늘 ·· 42
Tower of Babe 바벨탑 ······································ 44
Guest 손님 ·· 46
Vibrations 진동 ··· 48
Amplification 증폭 ·· 50
Spider's Web 거미 망 ······································· 52
November Street 11월의 거리 ························ 54
Thaw 해동 ·· 56
Your River 너의 강 ··· 58

Part III 제3부
On the Road 길 위에서

Champion 챔피언 ·· 62
Glasses 안경 ··· 64
Naked 알몸 ··· 66
Weight 무게 ·· 68
On the Road 길 위에서 ······································· 70
Dancing Silver Grass 춤추는 억새 ····················· 72
Problem 문제 ··· 74
Raindrops 빗방울 ·· 76
The Dance of Fairies 요정의 춤 ························ 78
Mysterious Power 신비한 힘 ······························ 80
Curiosity 호기심 ·· 82

Part IV 제4부
Whistling 휘파람

Whistling 휘파람 ················· 86
A Gentle Breeze 미풍 ················· 88
Drifter 떠돌이 ················· 90
Hands and Arms 손과 팔 ················· 92
A Rift 갈라진 틈 ················· 94
Winter Stream 겨울 냇물 ················· 96
Invigoration 활력 ················· 98
Limitations 한계 ················· 100
Unbroken Order 중단없는 순서 ················· 102
Fashionable Winds 풍조 ················· 104
The Tropic of Capricorn 동지선 ················· 106

Part V 제5부

Seizing Time 시간 잡기

Resentment 원망 ·················· 110
Intention 의도 ·················· 112
The Rising Star 떠오를 별 ·················· 114
Net 그물 ·················· 116
Genetic Code 유전 암호 ·················· 118
A Lost Person 길 잃은 사람 ·················· 120
Seizing Time 시간 잡기 ·················· 122
Eyes and Ears 눈과 귀 ·················· 124
Messenger of Time 시간의 전령 ·················· 126
Spring Snow 봄눈 ·················· 128
The X-Factor 미지의 요인 ·················· 130

Epilogue 에필로그

Unseen, Yet Present 안 보이지만 ·················· 132

About the Author 글쓴이 ····························· 134

| Prologue **|**

Beyond the Fence

One step beyond the fence,
I dare to venture forth.
In one hand, a stethoscope,
In the other, a telescope.

Following the pulse and breath
I trace the source,
Yearning to glimpse the origin,
With eyes full of longing and dreams.

Galileo's telescope,
Opened the night sky of the 16th century.
Now, the infrared telescope
Stands at the threshold of the Big Bang.

The more we unveil the mystery,
The more wondrous it becomes.
The more we overcome the miracles,
The more marvelous it grows.

| 프롤로그 |

울타리 밖

울타리 밖으로 한 발짝
더 나아가 보려나
한 손에 청진기
다른 손에 망원경

박동과 숨소리 따라
원천을 더듬으며
기원을 엿보려는
꿈과 동경의 눈빛이지

갈릴레오의 망원경은
16세기 밤하늘을 열었지
적외선 망원경은 지금
빅뱅의 문턱을 서성대지

신비는 벗길수록
더욱 놀라워지고
기적은 넘을수록
더욱 경이로우리

제 1 부
성취

Part I
Achievement

Achievement

Eyes that gazed upon
The winter sunset at sea,
Entreating the splendor of tomorrow,
Now behold the river
of abundance,
Brimful with the breath of spring.

Across the sea and
Over the mountains,
The radiance of spring
Will soon cover the world,
The fulfillment of the promise
Will be unstoppable.

Yet in today's eyes,
Does the gaze of yesterday
Still linger?
Wouldn't the gift be mistaken
For one's own achievement?
The abundance for one's own boast?

성취

겨울 바다 낙조를
응시하던 눈
내일의 영화를
못내 간구하더니
이제 봄기운 넘치는
풍요의 강을 보네

바다를 건너서
산을 넘어
봄의 광채가 곧
세상을 덮으리
약속의 실현은
거침이 없으리

오늘의 눈엔 아직도
어제의 응시가
살아가고 있는지
선물을 자기 성취로
풍요를 제 자랑으로
오해하진 않겠는지

Sensor

All we see is
Flowing water,
Swaying trees in the breeze.
All we hear are
Cicadas singing,
And the wind whispering through the leaves.

Are we trying to
Fill or empty?
To grasp or let go?
Are we still
Undecided?
Or perhaps both?

What we see is never the whole picture,
And what we hear is always subjective..
Where do we stand in this moment?
Are our sensors accurate?
Who checks the sensors, and
Who owns the sensors?

센서

보이는 건
흐르는 물
흔들리는 나무
들리는 건
매미 소리
바람 소리

채우려는지
비우려는지
잡으려는지
놓으려는지
아직도 미정인지
둘 다 다인지

보이는 게 어찌 다 같으랴
들리는 것도 서로 다르리
지금 어디에 서 있지
우리의 센서는 정확한지
센서는 누가 점검하는지
누가 센서의 주인인지

Human and Beast

In a world that passes us by
Without a second glance,
You stopped for me and
Allowed me to cross the path.
Who told you to do that?
Did you pity me?

I waved hello,
Even if we don't see each other's faces,
You must have acknowledge me
In the depths of your heart..
As we are strangers to each other,
The world is not just about rewards.

Humans and beasts,
Live in the same cage,
So our conflict will never end.
Today, the human won,
I hope it will always be so,
But I know that's not likely.

사람과 짐승

거들떠보지도 않고 그저
스쳐 지나가는 세상에서
유독 제 갈 길을 멈추고
내 길을 건너게 해준 이
누가 그리하라 했는지
불쌍히 여겨져서이리

손을 흔들어 인사를 하지
서로 누군지 안 보여도
그도 내가 누군지 모르면서
마음 깊이선 답례했으리
서로 생면부지이니
세상이 보상만은 아니리

사람과 짐승이
한 우리에 살고 있으니
싸움 그칠 날 없으리
오늘은 사람이 이겼지
늘 그러길 바라지만
늘 그러긴 어려우리

Intuition

Don't be afraid of the knocking sound,
Don't miss the opportunity that opens,
Don't run away in fear.

What's truly precious
Is what your gut tells you,
Intuition comes first,
Logic comes later.

Transcendental intuition,
Is the greatest gift of all.
When it calls, when it opens,
Why hesitate for a moment?

It's open to you by choice,
So enter without doubt
And hold on to the precious gift.

직감

두드리는 소리를 두려워 마시게
열려오는 기회를 놓치지 말아야지
무서워 뒷걸음쳐 도망가지 마시게

아주 값진 걸
붙드는 건
직감이 먼저이지
논리는 나중이지

초월적 직감은
선물 중 가장 큰 선물
부를 때 열릴 때
어찌 분초를 주저하리

택하여 문을 열어주는 거리
두렴 없이 믿고 들어가
귀중한 선물을 꽉 잡아야지

The Void

In the depths of silence,
Listen to the wondrous stillness.
Here, at the apex of all,
A new journey begins.

The void, unblemished and pure,
Is a vessel of astonishing beauty,
A pristine and perfect shore.

The space of purity is a sacred domain,
Where all is concentrated,
A balanced space-time,
A realm of dynamic order.

허공

침묵의 깊은 속에서
놀라운 고요를 듣지
여기의 정점은
거기의 출발점이지

공허는 불순물이 제거된
놀랍게 아름다운
완전 순수의 장이지

순수의 장은 거룩한 장
모두가 집중되고
균형 잡힌 시공
역동적 질서의 장이지

The Mysterious Forest

Sent to do so,
No matter how
You try to escape,
You will do it.

It is given and then taken away,
And sometimes given again.

Though some say they can't,
There are those who can do it well,
Some boast that they can do it
Only to end up in failure.

It is taken away and then given back,
And sometimes taken away again.

It is a mysterious forest
Full of great significance.
It will be an endless journey
To explore it.

신비의 숲

그렇게 하도록
보내졌기에
아무리 도망치려 해도
그걸 하게 되리

주었다가도 빼앗고
다시 주기도 하지

못한다고 사양하지만
잘 해낼 자가 있고
할 수 있다고 뽐내지만
망쳐놓는 이 있지

빼앗았다가도 주고
다시 빼앗기도 하리

큰 뜻이 담긴
신비의 숲이지
한없이 헤쳐갈
답사가 되겠지

Reaction

Even though you received such grace,
Why is the reaction so slow?
Perhaps it's difficult to handle,
It may require time to digest.

The reaction will surely
Manifest itself.
Though outwardly unresponsive,
Traces will be left within.

Becoming latent reactions,
In a different direction,
Riding the chain of events,
Sparks will eventually fly.

Reacting invisibly,
In the world,
There are
Far too many.

반응

그렇게 은혜를 받았는데
반응이 왜 이리도 느리지
감당키 어려워서인지
소화 시간이 필요하리

반응은 분명
드러나게 되리
겉은 무반응이나
안에 흔적을 내리

잠재 반응이 되어
다른 방향으로
연속 사슬을 타고
불꽃을 튀기게 되리

보이지 않게
반응하는 게
세상에는
너무나 많지

Transcendence

The once trapped heart,
Unbeknownst to even myself,
Will surely be liberated.

It's not surrender,
But transcendence.
Casting off evil,
And embracing virtue.

It's not surrender,
But a shout of triumph.
Throwing away defilement,
And donning holy robes.

In the dazzling light,
A remarkable peace
Will flow into the heart.

초월

갇혔던 가슴이
저도 모르는 사이
후련히 풀려지리

포기가 아니라
초월이지
악을 버리고
선을 붙들었지

항복이 아니라
개선의 함성이지
모독을 벗어 던지고
거룩한 옷을 입었지

눈 부신 빛 가운데
놀라운 평화가
가슴에 흘러들지

Small Joys

The small joys of everyday life
Shall grow with great strength,
Supporting the crumbling sky
And sustaining it from falling apart.

Small worries
Grow into great despair,
But small joys
Drive away immense despair.

The savior
Is always nearby,
Waiting for the moment
When you call out..

작은 기쁨

일상의 작은 기쁨이
큰 힘으로 자라올라
무너지려는 하늘을
떠받혀 지탱해 주리

작은 시름이
큰 절망으로 자라고
작은 기쁨이
큰 절망을 몰아내리

구원투수는
언제나 가까이서
부를 때를
기다리고 있지

Essential Desires

Feeling like you will live forever,
Don't be ashamed.
You may be worried that
You'll be scolded for doing so,
Since you are still a child and immature.

That's how you were born,
And that's the essence of life.
All strength comes from there,
All hope resides within,
All longing is its testament.

To protect your dignity,
As if you've gained enlightenment,
Don't try to extinguish the rising flames,
Don't try to stop the blowing wind.
Believing in eternity, it shall be eternal.

본질적 욕구

영원히 살 것 같은 기분
부끄러워 마시게
아직 어린애라
철이 안 들어 그렇다고
핀잔 들을까 눈치 보시지

그렇게 태어났고
그게 생명의 본질이지
모든 힘이 거기서 나오리
모든 희망이 그 안에 있지
모든 갈망이 그 증표이지

체신 지키느라
득도나 한 것처럼
솟는 불길을 끄려 마시게
부는 바람을 막지 마시게
영원을 믿으니 영원하리

Bound and Entangled

Seems like we've stopped,
But we can't really stop at all.
Once entwined with each other,
We won't be completely disconnected.

The nature of being bound, who can tell?
The power of unity, indeed, is astonishing.
Everyone might guess but still,
The reason remains elusive.

Thought we'd never see each other again,
Yet here we are, meeting once more.
Run away, but it's still within the Earth,
Disappear, but still within the universe.

What being entangled means, who knows?
It' a mysterious network.
Tracking tirelessly without pause,
Yet the cause remains not captured.

묶임과 얽힘

아주 그만둔 건 아니네
전혀 그만둘 수야 없지
한번 서로 맺어진 건
완전히 끊어지지 않으리

묶임이 어떤 건지 알리
결속의 위력은 놀랍지
누구나 짐작은 하지만
왜인지는 아직 모르리

더는 못 볼 것 같더니
서로 다시 만나게 되네
달아나 봐야 지구 안이지
사라져 봐야 우주 안이지

얽힘이 무언지는 알리
불가사의한 네트워크지
추적은 무던히 하지만
까닭은 아직 안 잡히리

제 2 부
해동

Part II
Thaw

Milestone

From the high and
Blue sky I look up,
Something seeps in
And settles deep in my heart.

Along with my breath,
May comfort rise,
And in time with my heartbeat,
May vitality overflow.

The shadow of time
Wavers on the path.
What dreams do you hold?
Where is the next milestone set?

The forest will sway in the wind,
The river will hasten its flow.
Is there a guide
To navigate the whirlpools?

이정표

눈을 들어 바라보는
높고 푸른 하늘에서
무언가 스며들어와
가슴 깊이 둥지를 틀지

숨결을 따라서
위로가 차오르리
박동에 맞추어
활기가 넘치길

시간의 그림자가
길 위에서 흔들리지
무슨 꿈을 꾸고 있지
다음 이정표는 짰는지

숲이 바람에 휘둘리리
강이 흐름을 재촉하리
소용돌이를 헤쳐 나갈
길잡이는 마련되었는지

Passing Through the Tunnel

Don't be afraid,
My child,

This is just a tunnel
That we're passing through.

Hold my hand tightly,
And nestle in my arms,

Soon the darkness will fade,
And a dazzling world will unfold.

터널 통과

아가야
무서워 마라

잠시 지나가는
터널이란다

내 손 꼭 붙잡고
내 품에 안겨

곧 어둠은 사라지고
눈부신 나라가 열려

Shadow

What kind of shadow is this,
On a sunny day like this?
Your eyes and smile
Are cast in shadow.

Is there a place in this world
Where there is no shadow?
A hidden shade,
A shadow you cast yourself.

The shadow falls
Depending on the angle of the light,
And it is peeled away
Depending on the place you stand.

A small shadow
Hides a great joy,
And even a large shadow
Can be swept away by a small joy.

What waits to be revealed
Within your shadow?
Within my shadow,
Someone will beg for it to fall.

그늘

어인 그늘인지
경사의 날인데
눈빛과 미소에
그늘이 져 있어

그늘 안 진 곳이
이 세상에 있으랴
가려진 그늘
스스로 가린 그늘

빛의 각도에 따라
그늘이 지고
서는 장소에 맞춰
벗겨져 가리

작은 그늘에
큰 기쁨이 가려지고
큰 그늘도
작은 기쁨이 걷어내리

네 그늘 안에서는
무엇이 벗겨질 때를 기다리지
내 그늘 안에서는
누군가 벗겨질 때를 간구하리

Tower of Babel

Already a great being,
But still not realizing,
To prove their abilities,
They climb high to reveal their name,
And try to seize the throne of heaven.

How high will they build the tower?
No matter how high they climb and climb,
There will always be another sky above.

Though judged by grace*
To prevent union through sin,
The dream of Babel still lingers,
Staying up all night inside me,
Secretly building the tower.

* Genesis 11:9.

바벨탑

이미 위대한 존재인데
아직 못 깨달아서이리
제 능력을 증명해 보이려
높이 올라가 이름을 드러내려
하늘의 왕좌까지 찬탈하려나

얼마나 높이 탑을 쌓으려나
아무리 높이 오르고 또 올라도
그 위에 또 하늘이 언제나 있지

죄악으로 연합 못하도록
은혜의 심판을 받았어도*
바벨의 꿈은 호시탐탐하리
아직도 몰래 탑을 쌓느라
내 안에서 밤을 지새우지

* 창세기 11:9.

Guest

Whether you like it or not,
Whether it matches your thoughts or not,
Whether you acknowledge it or not,
The world turns this way.

Already in the past,
From that very distant time,
The world has always been this way.
It will be this way in the future.

Just because you say it's beautiful,
Just because you agree it's worthwhile,
The world will not follow suit.
You are just a passing guest.

손님

마음에 들건 말건
생각과 같건 않건
네가 인정하든 말든
세상은 이처럼 돌아가리

이미 벌써 예전
아주 먼 그때부터
세상은 본시 이러해
앞으로도 이럴 거야

네가 아름답다고 해서
보람 있다고 동의해서
세상이 따라 하지 않으리
너는 지나가는 손님이지

Vibration

Eyes fixed on the other side,
His face occasionally
Flickers with a peculiar vibration.

As his tremors stir me within,
Do I see what he sees?

The wind draws something on the river,
In a world where all share the vibration,
They must have exchanged information.

Someone will see what I see,
My vibration will shake someone.

진동

눈은 강 건너에 고정되고
그의 얼굴에는 가끔
야릇한 진동이 스쳐 가지

그의 진동이 내 안을 흔드니
그가 보는 걸 나도 보는지

바람이 강물에 무언갈 그리지
모두 진동을 공유하는 세상이니
서로의 정보를 교환했으리

내가 보는 걸 누군가도 보리
내 안의 진동이 누군갈 흔들리

Amplification

There will be a day when
Your heart and mind
Become as small as a bean,
Smaller than a grain of sesame.

Trembling and falling into despair
Is to amplify the joy that is to come.
It is to maximize your potential.
If you don't lose your way, you will be fine.

The whole world was born
From the smallest seed.
Since it has shrunk to its minimum,
It's time to grow to its maximum.

증폭

마음과 생각이
콩알만 하게
깨알보다 작게
되는 날이 있지

떨리고 비탄에 빠지는 것은
맞게 될 환희를 증폭하려 서지
잠재력을 최대화해 주려 서리
방향만 안 놓치면 제대로 되리

가장 작은 알맹이에서
온 세상이 태어나왔지
줄어들 대로 줄어들었으니
커질 대로 커질 때를 맞으리

Spider's Web

Up and down the line,
The spider busily weaves its web.
Learned or innate,
It does not doubt its own prowess.

In the universe, a cosmic web,
In the brain, a neural web,
In the world, an internet web,
In the quantum realm, a quantum web.

Not only greed and envy,
Not only destruction,
It is also a web that raises,
Nourishes, and harvests.

There is no place without a spider's web,
Visible or not, they intertwine,
Feeding each other, laughing and crying,
Spreading in all directions.

거미 망

줄을 타고 쥐었다 폈다
거미가 망 짓기에 바쁘리
배웠는지 타고났는지
자신만만 두렴도 없지

우주에는 우주 망
뇌 안에는 뇌 망
세상엔 인터넷망
퀀텀 세계엔 퀀텀 망

탐욕과 시기와
파괴뿐만은 아니리
일으키고 베풀고
거두는 망이기도 하리

거미 망 없는 데는 없으리
보이게 안 보이게 모두
서로 먹고 살며 웃고 울게
사방팔방 엮어 벌려놓았으리

November Street

Down the foggy November street,
Fallen leaves dance unceasingly.
I wish the colors were deeper,
But who can stop the urging of time?

Even though you will never be abandoned,
You feel anxious about what might happen if it is.
This is especially true in the transitional season.

You must forget something,
There is always a next.
You must be shaken by something,
You are not alone anywhere.

Just once won't be enough,
You must remind yourself often,
Especially in the transitional time.

11월 거리

안개 자욱한 11월 거리로
그침 없이 단풍이 날리지
빛깔이 더 짙으면 좋으련만
시간의 재촉을 누가 막으랴

결코 안 버려질 텐데도
그렇게 되면 어쩌나 초조하리
환절기엔 더욱 그러하리

무언갈 깜박해 서지
언제나 다음이 있는걸
무언가에 흔들려 서리
어디서나 홀로가 아닌걸

결코 한 번으론 안 되리
자주 일깨워 주어야지
환절기엔 더욱 그러하리

Thaw

The sky is already spring,
But the ground is still winter.

A bird cawing loudly
Crouching on a riverside tree,
Resenting the slow spring.

When the inside is frozen,
The outside will no thaw.

What can you hold
With a clenched fist?
You must first untie the knot.

How can you greet a elegant smile
With a frowning face full of anger?

Even so, that day will come someday.
A hand greater than you
Will create a time within you.

The light from the sky will shine
And melt the frozen ground.

해동

하늘은 이미 봄인데
땅은 아직 겨울이네

깍깍 울부짖는 새
냇가 나무에 웅크려
더딘 봄을 원망하리

안이 얼어붙었으니
밖이 안 풀려가리

움켜쥔 주먹으로
무얼 잡을 수 있으랴
꼬인 걸 먼저 풀어야지

찌푸린 성난 얼굴로 어찌
우아한 미소를 맞아들이리

그래도 언젠간 그날은 오리
너보다 큰 너그러운 손이
네 안에 때를 만들어 주리

하늘빛을 쪼여서
언 땅을 녹여주리

Your River

Why am I here again today,
Standing by the river?
Where is your river flowing
Right now?

It seems to have countless branches,
But it will eventually become one stream.
It sounds like countless voices,
But it really comes from one sound.

The currents are countless,
But they start from one place.
There are countless paths,
But they all lead to one place.

Tomorrow, you will surely
Stand by the river again.
From here will your river
Flow into what time?

너의 강

오늘도 왜인지
강가에 와 서 있지
너의 강은 지금
어디로 흐르는지

무수한 줄기로 보이지만
결국 한줄기로 들게 되리
무수한 소리로 들리지만
실은 한소리에서 왔지

흐름은 무수하지만
한군데서 시작되지
길은 수없이 많으나
한군데로 들어가리

내일도 분명
강가에 서게 되리
너의 강은 여기서
어느 때로 흘러들지

제 3 부
길 위에서

Part III
On the Road

Champion

In the human mind,
Man reigns as champion,
But the beast lies in wait,
And the angel also resides.

When the weather grows harsh
And man's spirit wanes,
A championship title match
Will take place in the square ring.
May the angel triumph,
But the counterattack of the hungry beasts
Will be ruthless and fearsome.

The weather is capricious,
And the foe is formidable,
Thus, maintaining the championship
Will never be an easy feat.

챔피언

인간의 두뇌에서는
사람이 챔피언이지만
짐승이 도사려 있고
천사도 같이 살지

날씨가 사나워져
사람의 기가 쇠진할 땐
챔피언 띠를 걸고
사각의 링이 벌어지리
천사가 이기면 좋으련만
굶주린 짐승들의 역공이
무자비하고 무서우리

날씨는 무상하고
적수가 만만치 않으니
챔피언 유지하기가
늘 쉽지만은 않으리

Glasses

All I see are the swaying
Bare branches of November.
I wipe my frosty glasses
And in a crevice, a single rose
Greets me with a radiant smile.

How many people are
Trapped in the world
Filtered by their glasses?

They will weep and cry,
Mistakenly believing
That astonishingly beautiful things
Do not exist because
They cannot see them.

안경

보이는 건 휘둘리는
조락의 11월 가지들뿐
서리 낀 안경을 닦아내니
틈새에 핀 한 송이 장미
화려한 미소로 맞는다

얼마나 많은 이가
안경이 걸러내 주는
세상에 갇혀 사는지

안경 안의 세상을
우주 전부로 알지
놀랍게 아름다운 것들
안 보이니 없는 걸로
잘못 알고 울부짖으리

Naked

Even when trying to cover,
It ends up being exposed.
And when attempting to reveal,
It becomes impossible.

Struggling to conceal,
One is tormented by nightmares.
Eager to uncover,
The mind plunges into confusion.

What chases so,
That the spine turns cold?
Looking around, there's no one,
Only the sound of dragging feet.

A whirlwind blows,
Leaves fluttering in the air.
A self-portrait, stripped bare,
Whirls in the vortex.

알몸

가리려 해도
드러나게 되고
드러내려 해도
안되는 세상

가리려 애쓰니
악몽에 시달리리
드러내려 조바심치니
뇌가 혼선에 빠지리

무엇에 쫓기기에
등골이 서늘해지지
둘러보나 아무도 없고
질질 끄는 발소리뿐

회오리바람이 불지
가랑잎이 휘날리지
알몸이 된 자화상이
소용돌이를 치고 있지

Weight

Do you feel your own weight?
It's time for a thorough inspection,
Inside and out, with great care.

Too light, you'll be blown away,
If you're too heavy,
You'll collapse and fall.
Standing on a steep slope,
This becomes even more true.

Sometimes we forget,
That the world is relative.
It's time to just look at me and run.

Why do you close the door
Because you don't see it?
How bright your eyes truly are.
Feelings come from touch,
But often, we're caught unaware.

무게

제 무게를 느끼는지
안과 밖을 두루
살필 때가 온 거리

너무 가벼우면 날려가고
지나치게 무거우면
제물에 쓰러지게 되리
비탈길에 서 있으면
더욱 그렇게 되어 가리

세상이 상대적인걸
까맣게 잊을 때가 있지
저만 보고 달려갈 때리

안 보인다고 문을 닫는지
네 눈이 얼마나 밝다고
느낌은 닿음에서 오리
그러나 자주 우리는
잡힌 줄 모르게 잡혀 있지

On the Road

Because I came from beyond,
I gaze upon that place.
Though unseen and unheard,
It touches my heart, drawing me near,
I lean towards it always.

A hidden network,
With a mysterious wireless communication,
We must be connected.
Countless wondrous messages
Ascend and descend without number.

Caught in wonder and awe,
Following the signals sent,
Countless veils of mystery,
I lift one by one,
Climbing endlessly upwards.

We are all
On the road of
Insatiable longing
Towards the beyond,
We live with it in our hearts.

길 위에서

너머에서 왔기에
거기를 바라보리
안 보이고 안 들리지만
마음에 닿아 끌기에
늘 거기로 기울이지

숨어 있는 네트워크
오묘한 무선통신으로
서로 연결되어 있으리
놀라운 메시지가 수없이
위아래를 오르내리지

경이와 경외에 잡혀
보내오는 신호를 따라
무수히 가려진 신비의
장막을 하나씩 들치며
한없이 위로 기어오르지

우리는 모두
저 너머를 향한
채울 수 없는
갈망의 길 위에서
그리움을 품고 살아가리

Dancing Silver Grass

In the windy riverside meadow,
The silver grass dance is in full swing.
They sway back and forth, up and down,
Drawing or writing something.

Are they drawing a picture on the ground?
Writing numbers on the water?
Or are they writing a message in the sky?
The topic and target would be appropriate.

You are here now,
What are you drawing?
Where am I sending
What signal?

춤추는 억새

바람 부는 냇가 동산에서
억새 춤이 한창 벌어지지
앞뒤 아래위로 흔들어 대며
무언갈 그리는지 쓰는지

땅 위에 그림을 그리려나
물 위에 숫자를 적어두려나
하늘로 글을 써 올리려는지
주제와 대상은 적절하겠지

너는 지금 여기서
무얼 그려가고 있지
나는 어디로 무슨
신호를 보내고 있는지

Problem

Thirst and hunger,
What issue could there be?
Thanks to them,
We keep living on.

The problem lies
In the object and the goal,
Whether it is a means or an end,
It depends on that.

Spouting flames,
Cutting through the sky, soaring,
Where is it heading, what for,
Or whom is it rushing to meet?

The problem with desire
Is not the launch pad,
But the destination.
It's the difference between heaven and earth.

문제

목마르고 배고픈 게
무슨 문제이겠나
그 덕분에
살아가고 있지

대상과 목표가
문제겠지
수단인지 목적인지
따라 달라지리

불꽃을 뿜어내며
하늘을 가르고 치솟는다
무얼 하러 어디로 가는지
누굴 만나러 달리는지

열망의 문제는
발사대이기보다
목표지점이겠지
하늘과 땅 차이지

Raindrops

Pressed under heavy clouds,
the sky touches the ground on this day,
The flow slows down,
And the surroundings become still.

This descending day
Is a time for contemplation.
The bare winter trees
Gaze distantly into the unknown.

What flowers they will bloom?
What fruits they will bear?
Their deliberations are underway,
Whether they meet the right time or not.

The early winter raindrops
Shatter on the surface of the stream,
In the heart that gazes upon them,
a strange ripple rises.

빗방울

덮인 구름에 눌려
하늘이 땅에 닿는 날
흐름은 느려지고
주위는 잠잠해지리

가라앉는 날은
묵상의 시간이지
스산한 동짓달 나무들이
멀거니 어딘갈 응시하지

어떤 꽃을 피울지
무슨 열매를 맺을지
심사숙고는 진행 중이리
때를 만나건 못 만나건

초겨울 빗방울이
냇물 위에 부서지지
바라보는 가슴에도
야릇한 물결이 일리

The Dance of Fairies

A dream so wondrous and absurd,
It refuses to leave my mind.
Is it a false signal received,
Or a glitch in the network?

Is my neural net too narrow,
Or is the cosmic web expanding too fast?
Is it due to the strange entanglement
Between my mind and the universe?

Why do waves of electrons and photons
Traverse the interstellar space?
What are gravitational waves trying to do
As they graze the horizon of my mind?

The solar wind intertwines with magnetic waves,
Creating an eerie aurora borealis.
This is not the work of demons or angels,
But surely the dance of mischievous fairies.

요정의 춤

너무나 놀랍고 황당한
꿈이 떠나가질 않으리
잘못 받은 신호인지
네트워크의 오작동일지

뇌 망이 너무 협소해선가
우주 망이 빨리 팽창하려나
뇌 망과 우주 망 사이의
기이한 얽힘 현상 때문인지

전자파와 광자 무리는 왜
성 간을 누비며 큰 파도 치는지
뇌 망의 지평을 스쳐 가면서
중력파는 무얼 하려는 건지

태양풍이 자기파와
어우러져 극광이 으스스하지
마귀는 아니고 천사도 아닌
장난꾸러기 요정들의 춤이겠지

Mysterious Power

At some point, for some reason,
you are suddenly overwhelmed by
an irresistible, mysterious power.

Your consciousness, caught in this power,
begins to resonate with a wondrous pulse
that transcends survival instinct.

Not self-generated, but drawn to
the mysterious power,
doors open at your touch.

Before you know it,
not you, but
the mysterious power lives within you.

Soon, the light of the incredible power
dwelling within you
begins to illuminate your surroundings.

Those around you
will notice before you do
that you are caught in the mysterious power.

신비한 힘

왜인지 어느 순간 갑자기
거역할 수 없는
신비한 힘에 압도되리

그 힘에 잡힌 의식이
생존본능을 넘어가는
놀라운 박동을 시작하리

자가발전이 아닌
신비한 힘에 끌리기에
손만 대면 문이 열리지

너도 모르는 사이
네 안에 네가 아니라
신비한 힘이 살아가리

어느새 안에 사는
경이로운 힘의 광채가
주위를 비추어 가리

신비한 힘에 잡힌걸
너보다도 더 먼저
주위가 알아차리지

Curiosity

To see is to hear,
To hear is to see.
A painting makes a sound,
A sound becomes a painting.

With each layer peeled back,
A new picture makes a sound.
With each page turned,
A strange sound becomes a painting.

With each peeling and turning,
You will encounter countless
Amazing and ecstatic worlds.
This is how you were led here.

Caught in wonder and awe,
Thirsting for the land of glory,
The soul of curiosity will continuously
Peel away the covered veil.

호기심

보는 것은 듣는 것이지
듣는 건 보는 것이지
그림이 소리를 내지
소리가 그림이 되리

한 겹 벗길 때마다
새 그림이 소리를 내지
한 장 넘길 때마다
낯선 소리 그림이 보이리

벗기고 넘길 때마다
놀랍고 황홀한 세계를
수없이 만나게 되리
이리하도록 이끌었으리

경이와 경외에 잡혀
영광의 나라에 목말라
호기심의 혼은 끊임없이
가려진 막을 벗겨 나가리

제 4 부
휘파람

Part IV
Whistling

Whistling

In an unexpected moment,
Out of nowhere,
Comes the sound of a whistle.

I wake up and look outside,
A meteor shower is in full swing.
Riding on the whistle,
A message flies in.

It's filled to the brim
With letters or symbols,
Clearly, it's an important notice.

I look it over carefully,
And I can guess who sent it,
But I'm still unable
To decipher it.

Blowing the whistle to wake me up,
Revealing the wonder of the meteor shower,
It's trying to open the eyes of my soul.

휘파람

어느 땐데
난데없이
휘파람 소리이지

잠이 깨어 내다보니
유성우가 한창이네
휘파람을 타고
메시지가 날아들지

글씨인지 부호인지
가득히 메워진 걸 보니
분명 중요한 통보이리

이리저리 살펴보니
누가 보내는지는
짐작 가는데 아직
판독은 못 하고 있지

휘파람을 불어 깨워대며
유성우의 경이를 드러내어
심령의 눈을 밝혀 가려나

A Gentle Breeze

Cutting through the heat,
A gentle breeze wafts by.
After passing the hurdle
It's a welcome descent.

It could be a messenger from someone,
But in this mutable world, doubt comes first.
Whether we expect, ignore, or refuse,
What comes will come and what goes will go.
The time will soon come when dragonfly
Will soar high and the cicadas will run wild.

Looking up at the sky, we can see the time,
And by examining the earth, we may find good fortune.
But if we only look at the earth, we'll miss the time,
And if we only look at the sky, we'll stumble and fall.

미풍

무더위를 가르며
미풍이 불어오지
고비를 넘기니
내림 길이지

누군가 보내는 전령일 텐데
무상한 세상 의심이 앞서리
기대하든 무심하든 거부하든
올 것은 오고 갈 것은 가리
잠자리가 곧 높이 떠 오르고
매미가 기승부릴 때가 오리

하늘을 바라보면 때를 알리
땅을 살피다 횡재할 수 있지
땅만 바라보단 때를 놓치리
하늘만 쳐다보니 걸려 넘어지리

Drifter

Rather than offering,
I put myself forward,
Thus receiving no praise.

Competition turns to envy,
Anger to duel,
Escalating to the peak.

We raise the flag of rebellion,
Because we are reigned by
What we should rule.

Being dragged into slavery
By the stone we carved,
We become restless drifters.

떠돌이

바치기보다
내세웠기에
칭찬을 못 받지

경쟁이 시기로
분노가 결투로
치닫지

다스려야 할 것에
지배당하기에
반역의 깃발을 올리지

제가 깎아 세운 돌에
노예로 끌리며
초조한 떠돌이가 되지

Hands and Arms

Running along the forest path by the stream,
A figure in black with a red hat
Raises the arms high, reaching for the sky,
Eagerly swinging diligently to and fro
To embrace a generous gift.

Seeing that the motions have ceased,
She must have embraced what she desired.
Whether it was given or snatched,
Or merely pretending to have received it
With an empty heart.

Hands spread out to grasp,
Arms opened to embrace,
Whoever or whatever it is,
It must have already been embraced,
Whether it's real or an illusion.

손과 팔

냇가 숲길을 달리는
검은 옷의 빨간 모자
팔을 높이 치켜올려
한 아름 안아 들이려
부지런히 휘두르지

움직임이 그친 걸 보니
원하는 걸 안았으리
주는 걸 받은 건지
가로채 뺏은 건지
받은 척 빈 가슴인지

잡으려 펼친 손
안으려 벌린 팔
누군지 무엇인지
이미 잡아 안았으리
실상이든 허상이든

A Rift

On whom shall I pour out
the expanded pressure gas?
In order to avoid the implosion,
shall I erupt boiling lava?

The world is a history of wounds and healing.
The essence of healing is
To turn vicious cycles into virtuous ones,
And to manage the source of wounds.

We must drain the pus and
Calm the anger of the wound,
Bandage it so that new flesh can grow,
And heal the rift.

갈라진 틈

팽창된 압력가스를
누구에 쏟아부으려나
내 파를 모면하려니
들끓는 용암을 분출하리

세상은 상처와 치유의 역사
치유의 진수는
악순환을 선순환으로
상처의 원천 다스리기

고름을 빼내 상처의
분노를 가라앉히고
새살이 돋게 싸매야지
갈라진 틈을 아물려야지

Winter Stream

Winter sunlight and cold wind
Are playing a seesaw game.
As if about to be covered with thin ice,
It scatters in the sunlit waves.

Each one will do their best,
And use their best strategy.
Will they engrave this opportunity,
Which may not come again,
As an immortal moment?
It is a very beautiful picture,
Not too obsessed with winning or losing.

The world does not always
Turn out the way you want it to.
It may give you something better,
But you may not know it and sigh.

겨울 냇물

겨울 햇살과 찬바람이
시소게임을 한창 벌이네
살얼음이 덮여 가려는 듯
햇살 받은 물결에 흩어지지

각기 받은 기량을 다하리
최상의 책략을 발휘하리
다시 올지 모를 이 기회를
불후의 순간으로 새기려나
승부에 너무 집착하지 않는
아주 멋진 한 폭의 그림이네

열망하는 대로 세상은
이루어지는 건 아니리
더 좋은 다른 걸 주었는데
알아 못 채고 한숨지으리

Invigoration

As the warm sunlight descends,
Life stirs by the snow-covered stream,
Vigor bursts forth with a vibrant gleam.

Intertwined branches reach high,
Swaying towards the dazzling sky,
Eagerly grasping the moment of hope.

Sun, wind, and water, all in accord,
Prepare to seize what's yet to be explored.
From where does this vitality spring?

The world is a stage for receiving.
"Seek, and you shall receive," they sing.
May their convictions be firm and unwavering.

For by its grace, the world shall rise,
Overcoming the harsh winter night.
Awakening to a new dawn's light.

활력

햇빛이 포근히 내리니
눈 덮인 냇가에 어느새
활기가 무럭무럭 나네

가지들이 손에 손을 모아
눈부신 하늘 높이 흔들지
소망의 때를 움켜쥐려네

해도 바람도 냇물도
무언갈 잡을 태세이네
어디서 솟는 활력인지

세상은 받을 자세의 무대
"구하면 받게 되리라"
다져진 확신이길 바라지

그 덕분에 세상은
혹독한 겨울밤을
이기고 깨어나리

Limitations

Though we may pierce deeply
And examine closely,
Our understanding is limited.

Countless mistaken
Perceptions distort
The world around us.

Myriad delusions
And misunderstandings
Bring us sorrow.

Until we acknowledge
The inescapable boundaries of our knowledge,
We will remain trapped within the confines of
our own limitations.

한계

멀리 깊이
면밀하게
꿰뚫는다지만

수없이 많은
잘못된 인식이
세상을 왜곡하리

수많은
착각과 오해가
우리를 비통케 하리

넘을 수 없는
우리의 한계를
알아챌 때까지

Unbroken Order

Bound by the illusion of the present,
We dedicate our lives to it.
Ultimately, it shatters and fades,
Leading us to the next moment.

The order of time
Is designed for us to live
In the present.
So we shall live accordingly.

The order of space
Was created for a reason.
There is surely a deeper meaning
Within it.

Unbroken order,
Endless connection.
Within it,
We are driven to live.

중단없는 순서

현재의 환상에 잡혀
모두를 바쳐 살게 하리
드디어 부서져 사라져서
다음 순서로 들어가지

시간의 순서
현재에 살도록
디자인되었으니
그렇게 살아가리

공간의 순서
그렇게 지은 건
그 안에 분명
깊은 뜻이 있으리

중단 없는 순서
끝없는 연결
그 안에서
살게 하려서지

Fashionable Winds

With eyes clouded by the trend,
How can we lead the world?
With ears deaf to the current,
How can we build a nation?

All things worldly are currents of the times.
Adorned in the fashion of the day,
With words and actions following the flow,
We become mere packaging, fitting the trend.

Since all worldly affairs are relative,
Absolute truth is locked away in a closet.
Yet, perhaps it still has some value,
For we cannot completely discard it.

There is a sound to be heard.
Whose voice is it?
Do we cringe and hide?
Or do we run joyfully to embrace it?

풍조

풍조에 어두운 눈으로
어찌 세상을 이끌려나
세류를 못 타는 귀로
어찌 나라를 세워보려나

세상만사는 시대의 조류
풍조에 맞춰 화장하고
세류를 따라 언동을 꾸민
조류에 맞는 포장지라야지

세상사가 모두 상대성이니
절대 진리는 벽장에 갇혀있지
그래도 켕기는 데가 있는지
아주 버리지는 못하고 있지

들려오는 소리 있으리
누구의 목소리지
움찔하여 숨고 싶으냐
반가워 달려가 잡으려나

The Tropic of Capricorn

The wings of the sun
Flutter down to the Tropic of Capricorn.
The Southern Hemisphere, a land of passion.
The Northern Hemisphere, a season of rest.

Snowflakes whirl over mountains and fields.
As I rush to the horizon and gaze up at the sky,
Countless stars cascade down,
Adorning the stage of our gathering.
The prelude already echoes through the air.

The winter solstice is a starting point.
A deepening meditation,
A growing warmth of comfort.
A solidifying conviction.

동지선

태양의 날개가
동지선으로 날아들지
남반구는 열정의 나라
북반구는 휴게의 계절

산야에 눈발이 날리지
달려가 지평을 바라보니
쏟아져 내리는 별 무리네
함께할 무대를 장식하려나
전주곡이 벌써 울려 퍼지네

동지선은 시발점
깊어져 갈 명상
포근해 갈 위안
굳어져 갈 확신

제 5 부
시간 잡기

Part V
Seizing Time

Resentment

Triumph and joy,
Are mere specks of dust blown away.
Defeat and agony,
Are fleeting waves that pass by.

Not having received
Does not mean being forsaken.
Having already received,
Yet unknowingly holding resentment.

Photons carried by the wind
Pour down, covering mountains and rivers.
Life is all sustained by this,
Yet how many live knowing so?

Though you may not know,
There is something there.
There must be a reason for everything.
And so it was mean to be.

원망

승리와 환희
날려가는 티끌이지
패배와 고뇌
스쳐 가는 파도이지

받지 못했다고
버려진 건 아니리
이미 받았는데
모르고 원망하리

광자가 바람에 실려
강산을 덮어 쏟아지리
삶이 모두 이로 지탱되는데
얼마가 이를 알며 살아가는지

몰라도 있는 건 있지
매사에는 이유가 있으리
그것으로 충분하기에
그렇게 해 두었으리

Intention

If our intentions are good,
Are the results always good?

As we live helping others,
We may unknowingly,
Transcend our own selves.

As we help others,
Wishing to transcend ourselves,
We may transcend our own selves.

If the results are good,
Are our intentions also good?

의도

의도만 좋으면
결과는 다 좋은 건가

남을 돕고 살다 보면
저도 모르게
자기를 넘게도 되리

저를 넘고 싶어
남을 돕다 보면
저를 넘게도 되리

결과만 좋으면
의도도 다 좋은 건가

The Rising Star

Though it can not be seen now,
We eagerly gaze and listen
For the great star that will rise
Sooner or later.

Like reeds by the water's edge,
Swaying ceaselessly in the wind,
Our waiting eyes are fixed on the time.
Is it the assurance given by a promise?
Or the burning ambition of self-assertion?

Aren't we longing for
A star that has already passed by?
It may take millions of years
For the rising star to arrive here.

떠오를 별

지금은 안 보이지만
언젠간 떠오를 큰 별을
이제나저제나 애타게
내다보며 귀 기울이지

물가에 선 갈대 무리
끊임없이 바람에 휘둘리며
때를 기다리는 눈길
약속이 안겨준 확신인지
자기주장의 의기충천인지

이미 지나간 별을 이처럼
고대하는 건 아닐지
떠오를 별이 여기 오려면
천만년이 걸릴지도 모르리

Net

You must have been caught in an illusion
And lost your way,
While trying to get rid of the time and space
That were tailored to fit to your head and wings.

A small bird trapped in the net,
What did you believe in to reach this state?
Determined to break through the ceiling
And fly away,
You pushed yourself too hard,
Until your brain network burst open.
All the structural functions of your consciousness
Will spiral into panic.

Trying to escape the net of life,
The very foundation of existence,
You will be caught in the net of death.

그물

머리와 날개에 알맞게 맞춘
시공을 벗어보려 억지 쓰다
허상에 걸려 길을 잃었으리

그물에 걸린 작은 새야
무얼 믿다 이 지경이 되었지
천장을 깨고 날아 나가보려
오기로 밀어붙이다 보니
뇌 망이 터져 구멍이 났지
의식의 모든 구조기능이
연달아 공황에 빠져가리

생명의 기본 그물을
감금 장치인 줄 탈출하려다
죽음의 그물에 사로잡히지

Genetic Code

What are you gazing at
So intently?
Whom am I waiting for
With such a craned neck?

Inside our DNA,
The genes that gaze flutter,
The genes that wait breathe,
The gene of immortality is deeply embedded.

To recognize the signal,
To grasp the news,
To keep the promise,
We stare and wait.

The gene is a deeply engraved promise,
The signal is a call sent by the promise,
What is written will be fulfilled,
An indelible promise.

유전암호

너는 무얼 그렇게
뚫어지게 바라보는지
나는 누구를 이렇게
목을 빼어 기다리는지

우리의 DNA 안에는
바라보는 유전자가 퍼덕이지
기다리는 유전자가 숨 쉬지
영생 유전자가 깊이 새겨 있지

신호를 알아채려
소식을 붙들어
약속을 간직하려
바라보며 기다리리

유전자는 깊이 새겨 넣은 약속
신호는 약속이 보내는 부름
써넣은 대로 이루어지리
지워질 수 없는 약속이지

A Lost Person

It is not even a dark night,
Yet there is a lost person.
Have they been tempted astray?
Or have they stumbled and fallen?

There are many lost ones
On the path,
So how can we ask anyone
For directions?

If we follow their footsteps,
Without knowing where they are going,
Or what they are going to do,
We will likely lose our way too.

There is only one path,
A narrow path,
And it is not easy
To avoid getting lost.

Even on a bright spring day,
There are lost ones.
They are tempted to stray,
And they stumble and fall.

길 잃은 사람

짙은 밤도 아닌데
길 잃은 사람이 있지
유혹에 걸렸는지
실족하였는지

길 잃은 사람이
길 위에 많으니
아무에게나 어찌
길을 물으랴

어디로 가는지
무얼 하러 가는지
발자국만 따라가단
십상 길을 잃으리

오직 한길
좁은 길이니
잃지 않기
쉽지 않으리

화창한 봄날에도
길 잃은 사람이 있지
유혹에 걸려 서리
실족하여 서리

Seizing Time

It must have been
around this time,
You were trying to cross,
And I, to climb.

How rather than where,
And what rather than when,
Are told to be more important,
In seeking the meaning
Of the journey.

Crossing is all about
riding the waves.
Climbing is all about
seizing time.
Both are endless journeys.

Standing here now,
What is revealed?
How did I climb up?
What did you cross?

시간 잡기

그때가 아마도
이맘때 이리
너는 건너려 했고
나는 오르려 했으리

어디보다도
어떻게가
어느 때보다도
무엇인가가
더 의미 있다 하지

건너는 일은
파도타기
오르는 일은
시간 잡기
한없는 행진이지

지금 여기 서니
무엇이 드러나지
어떻게 올라왔는지
무얼 건너왔는지

Eyes and Ears

Don't grumble about the rough waves,
That's the place you dreamed of.
The groans of determination to do better
Are still proof of great expectations.

You cannot achieve it
With instinct alone.
You are swayed by instinct,
But don't stop there,
You have wings that will soar.

You have not only primal instincts,
But also transcendent abilities.
You have the eyes and ears
To recognize the signals coming down.

눈과 귀

풍파가 심하다고 투덜대지
그게 네가 꿈꾸던 그 자리지
더 잘해보려 다짐하는 신음
아직 기대가 큰 증거이지

본능만으로는
이루지 못하리
본능에 휘둘리지만
거기에 안 머물리
솟아오를 날개가 있지

원초적 본능뿐 아니라
초월적 능력도 있지
내리는 신호를 알아챌
눈과 귀를 갖추었지

Messenger of Time

Drawn by the sound of the wind,
Everyone must have gone out.
The fresh current
Seeps in.

If you look closely,
The witness of the season is already
Stirring to reveal itself
Between the branches.

What is beautiful is good
Just as it is.
As the buds burst open,
Joy will well up.

The messenger of time
Comes to plant spring.
Is the place where the buds will bloom
Prepared inside?

시간의 전령

바람 소리에 끌려
모두 나왔으리
신선한 흐름이
안으로 스며들리

자세히 살피면
계절의 증인이 벌써
가지 사이에 모습을
드러내려 꿈틀대리

보기 좋은 것은
그대로가 좋지
새싹이 터 나오니
반가움이 솟아오르리

시간의 전령이
봄을 심으러 오네
봉오리 필 자리는
안에 마련되었는지

Spring Snow

Carried by the sunlight,
Called by the northwest wind,
Snowflakes flutter down.
In the forest and the stream,
On the head and the heart,
Snowflakes settle down.

The moment they land,
The spring snow disappears,
It's pity that their delicate form doesn't last.
Surely they came here,
Carrying a mission,
Over the sea and across the river

The snowflake's wholehearted gesture,
Caught on the retina, travels through the circuits,
And ceaselessly knocks on the brain.
They are undoubtedly trying to convey
An important message, secretly without fail.
Will the mind's eye be able to perceive it?

봄눈

햇살에 실려
북서풍에 불려
눈발이 쏟아지지
숲에도 냇물에도
머리에도 가슴에도
눈송이가 내려앉는다

자리를 잡는 순간
사라지는 봄눈
정교한 모습이 아쉽지
분명 임무를 띠고
바다 넘어 강 건너
지금 여기에 왔으리

눈송이의 혼신 몸짓이
망막에 걸려 회로를 타고
뇌를 그침 없이 두드리리
틀림없이 중한 기별을
은밀히 전달하려는데
마음의 눈이 알아챌 건지

The X-Factor

When you are complacent in your abilities,
Your discernment becomes clouded.
You will often make mistakes.

If you lean to one side,
You will fall in that direction.
May it not be an endless fall.

Because you didn't have an experience
That touched your heart,
You lost the basics of discernment.
You will be deeply immersed in yourself.

The ants gather in swarms,
Busily preparing and bustling about,
Readying themselves for the impending monsoon.

As the unknown factor
Is hidden by arrogance,
You'll not able to see the signs of the times.

미지의 요인

능력에 자만하다 보니
분별력이 흐려져 가지
자주 실족하게 되리

쏠리면 기울어져
그쪽으로 쓰러지지
끝없는 추락 아니길

가슴 울린 체험이 없기에
분별의 기본을 잃었지
자기 안에 깊이 매몰되리

개미가 떼를 지어
동분서주하고 있지
다가올 장마를 대비하리

미지의 요인이
오만으로 가려지니
시대의 표적을 못 보리

| Epilogue |

Unseen, Yet Present

Unseen, yet present,
It dwells within.

A light waiting
In the darkness,
A joyful smile hidden
Within tears,
Eyes that sprout
From what has withered.

Unheard, yet alive,
It lives within.

The whisper of spring breeze
Crouching within winter,
A calling voice
From beyond the horizon,
The sound of a joyful pulse
Stirring the void.

｜에필로그｜

안 보이지만

안 보이지만
그 안에 있지

어둠 안에서
기다리는 빛
눈물 안에 숨긴
기쁨의 미소
시든 데서
돋아나는 눈

안 들리는데
그 안에 살지

겨울 안에 웅크린
봄바람 소리
지평 너머에서
불러대는 소리
공허를 흔드는
환희의 맥박 소리

About the Author

Lee Won-Ro

Poet as well as medical doctor (cardiologist), professor, chancellor of hospitals and university president, Lee Won-Ro`s career has been prominent in his brilliant literary activities along with his extensive experiences and contributions in medical science and practice.

Lee Won-Ro is the author of fifty two poetry books along with twelve anthologies. He also published extensively including ten books related to medicine both for professionals and general readership.

Lee Won-Ro`s poetic world pursues the fundamental themes with profound aesthetic enthusiasm. His work combines wisdom and knowledge derived from his scientific background with his artistic power stemming from creative imagination and astute intuition.

Lee Won-Ro`s verse embroiders refined tints and serene tones on the fabric of embellished words.

Poet Lee Won-Ro explores the universe in conjunction with his expertise in intellectual, affective and spiritual domains as a specialist in medicine and science to create his unique artistic world.

This book along with "Winter Gift", "Fair Winds", "Spiral Staircase", "The Watershed", "The Seed of Eternity", "Milky Way In DNA", "Signs of Recovery", "Applause", "Invitation", "Night Sky", "Revival", "The Promise", "Time Capsule", "The Tea Cup and the Sea", "The Tunnel of Waves", "The Tomorrow within Today", "Our Home", "The Sound of the Wind", "Flowers and Stars", "Red Berries", "Dialogue", "Corona Panic", "Chorus", "Waves", "Thanks and Empathy", "A Mural of Sounds", "Focal Point", "Day Break", "Prelude to a Pilgrimage", "Rehearsal", "TimeLapse Panorama", "Eve Celebration", "A Trumpet Call", "Right on Cue", "Why Do You Push My Back", "Space Walk", "Phoenix Parade", "The Vortex of Dances", "Pearling", "Priming Water", "A Glint of Light", "The River Unstoppable", "Song of Stars", "The Land of Floral Buds", "A Flute Player", "The Glow of a Firefly", "Resonance", "Wrinkles in Time", "Wedding Day", "Synapse", "Miracles are Everywhere", "Unity in Variety" and "Signal Hunter" are available at Amazon.com/author/leewonro or kdp.amazon.com/book shelf(paperbacks and e-books).

글쓴이

이원로

　시인이자 의사(심장전문의), 교수, 명예의료원장, 전 대학교 총장인 이원로 시인은 월간문학으로 등단, "빛과 소리를 넘어서", "햇빛 유난한 날에", "청진기와 망원경", "팬터마임", "피아니시모", "모자이크", "순간의 창", "바람의 지도", "우주의 배꼽", "시집가는 날", "시냅스", "기적은 어디에나", "화이부동", "신호추적자", "시간의 주름", "울림", "반딧불", "피리 부는 사람", "꽃눈나라", "별들의 노래", "멈출 수 없는 강물", "섬광", "마중물", "진주잡이", "춤의 소용돌이", "우주유영", "어찌 등을 미시나요", "불사조 행렬", "마침 좋은 때에", "나팔소리", "전야제", "타임랩스 파노라마", "장도의 서막", "새벽", "초점", "소리 벽화", "물결", "감사와 공감", "합창", "코로나 공황", "대화", "빨간 열매", "꽃과 별", "바람 소리", "우리집", "오늘 안의 내일", "파도의 터널", "찻잔과 바다", "타임캡슐", "약속", "소생", "밤하늘", "초대장", "박수갈채", "회복의 눈빛", "DNA 안 은하수", "영원의 씨", "분수령", "나선계단", "순풍", "겨울 선물" 등 54권의 시집과 13권의 시선집을 출간했다. 시집 외에도 그는 전공 분야의 교과서와 의학 정보를 일반인들에게 쉽게 전달하기 위한 실용서를 여러 권 집필했다.

이원로 시인의 시 세계에는 생명의 근원적 주제에 대한 탐색이 담겨져 있다. 그의 작품은 과학과 의학에서 유래된 지혜와 지식을 배경으로 기민한 통찰력과 상상력을 동원하여 진실하고 아름답고 영원한 우주를 추구하고 있다. 그의 시는 순화된 색조와 우아한 운율의 언어로 예술적 동경을 수놓아간다.

이원로 시인은 과학과 의학 전문가로서의 지성적, 감성적, 영적 경험을 바탕으로 그의 독특한 예술 세계를 개척해가고 있다.

이 시집을 비롯하여 "분수령", "영원의 씨", "DNA 안 은하수", "회복의 눈빛", "초대장", "밤하늘", "소생", "약속", "타임캡슐", "찻잔과 바다", "파도의 터널", "오늘 안의 내일", "우리집", "바람 소리", "꽃과 별", "빨간 열매", "대화", "코로나 공황", "합창", "물결", "감사와 공감", "소리 벽화", "초점", "새벽", "장도의 서막", "타임랩스 파노라마", "전야제", "나팔소리", "마침 좋은 때에", "어찌 등을 미시나요", "우주유영", "불사조 행렬", "춤의 소용돌이", "진주잡이", "마중물", "섬광", "멈출 수 없는 강물", "별들의 노래", "꽃눈 나라", "피리 부는 사람", "반딧불", "울림", "시집가는 날", "시냅스", "기적은 어디에나", "화이부동", "신호추적자", "시간의 주름" 등은 아래에서 구입할 수 있다.

Amazon.com/author/leewonro와 kdp.amazon.com/bookshelf(paperbacks and e-books)

길 위에서
On the Road

2024년 9월 20일 인쇄
2024년 9월 30일 발행

지은이 / 이원로
발행인 / 박진환
펴낸곳 / 조선문학사
등록번호 / 1-2733
주소 / 03730 서울 서대문구 통일로 389(홍제동)
대표전화 / 02-730-2255
팩스 / 02-723-9373
E-mail / chosunmh2@daum.net

ISBN 979-11-6354-309-1

정가 10,000원

* 인지는 저자와 합의 하에 생략
* 잘못된 책은 서점에서 교환해 드립니다.